I0095175

SOURED SMILES

By

Kunal Vyas

Published by:
Wildebeest Publishing Company, LLC
Syracuse, New York

Do you have a story to tell? What's your animal spirit? Share it with us. #hellobeesties
Copyright © 2024 by Kunal Vyas
You may visit the author's website at www.kunalvyas.com

Wildebeest
Publishing Co.

Wildebeest Publishing Company, LLC

All rights reserved, including the right to reproduce this book or portions thereof in any form. Unauthorized copying or distribution of the book is forbidden.

For more information about copyrights and usage, special discounts on bulk purchases, workshops, and engagements, please contact Wildebeest Publishing Company, LLC at (315) 220-0217, info@wildebeestpublishing.com, or online at www.wildebeestpublishing.com Wildebeest Publishing is dedicated to providing flexible remote work opportunities and has a presence in Syracuse, New York City, and Tampa

Wildebeest Publishing Company, LLC paperback First Edition February 2025, United States of America

Photographs property of Kunal Vyas

ISBN 978-1-958233-38-2 (Paperback)

LLCN

The publisher and artists can accept no legal responsibility for any consequences arising from the application of information, advice, or instructions given in this publication. The author, artists, and publisher have made all reasonable efforts to contact copyright holders for permission and apologize for any omissions or errors pertaining to credit for existing works. Corrections may be made to future versions. The opinions expressed in the book are those of the author and do not necessarily reflect the views of the publisher or the foreword author.

TABLE OF CONTENTS

FOREWORD

Not every smile in this world is as simple and beautiful as it seems. Just *dig* a bit deeper than the surface. Understanding the structure of the world we live in is *our* own responsibility — recognizing smiles is not a trivial part of it.

Often, we will realize that our lives are significantly different than they appear to us. At this point, our every action and, perhaps, smile will harbor diverse meanings. We will formulate, more intensely, unique and complicated personalities and perspectives; our own smiles will carry adjectives like *sweet* or *sour*.

Many things will influence our world of smiles — some, but not all, being pleasurable. Sometimes, smiles will try to hide *or inflict* various modes of pain. At times, smiles will be formal and artificial; at others, smiles will tell tales of triumph or victory. Perhaps, they will be a gift to the world, or they may be something to keep to ourselves.

I wonder: is our life simply a record of our vast, ponderous smiles? A while back, I published a book titled *Failed Frowns*. In that book, smiles were a *default* positive commodity; nonetheless, they are a *not-necessarily-positive* force in this book. This work explores the depth of various smiles and recognizes their diverse backgrounds.

Ask yourself: *what just made me smile?* It's a start.

1.
BITTERSWEET

Today, there was another note on the calendar for the planned absence of my regular caregiver. Usually, this means that I have no one to take me off my stiff, uncomfortable bed to use the restroom, brush, or even shower. My family members seldom have the strength to support me and, over time, have grown unfond of helping me accomplish tasks of daily living. What can I say? Life is just hard.

In 2001, my college education was cut short with a troublesome diagnosis of multiple sclerosis. Over 23 years later, the condition has left me bedridden, jobless, and immensely dependent. I rely heavily on caregivers to help me do even things such as getting to the toilet. As I understand it, it is extremely difficult to approach family for help; they are either too old and weak or belligerently moody. Ergo, my caregivers have become, I suppose, somewhat of a sustenance.

⚞╬╬⚟

Then, the story changed.

⚞╬╬⚟

Today was one of the few notable days when I, suddenly, was taken to my shower by a new and unplanned caregiver. I was happy with my fate, but it came and comes with costs [for me].

The man who showed up as my caregiver was a young-looking man from Cuba; luckily, I can communicate in Spanish. However, my voice is very weak, and I lose breath constantly while trying to get out what I am trying to say. In between gasps, I lose my audience.

Now, let me say a little more about myself. I grew up as my biggest fan. I dressed well, I thought. *I could make myself jealous of being me (if that makes any sense).* In 2001, bad luck visited me and gifted me with primary progressive multiple sclerosis, very long story shortened: in 2024, I require assistance to accomplish tasks of daily living (bathing, eating, toileting, etc.)

When taking me to shower, the following things happen: soap and shampoo are gathered by my caregiver; the shower water is turned warm; toothpaste is put in my mouth, and a toothbrush is given to me (I brush in the shower). After I finish brushing, I turn on the shower, and clean my mouth and wash the toothbrush.

Today, my brother was there to lightly guide the new caregiver. The caregiver, though, was sort of prepared and was aware of what needed to be done.

⚒

Here's where my self-pampering comes into play. Around the second or third year of high school, I began to pay closer attention to my physical appearance — specifically my hair. I spent significantly more time wherever I was able to see a reflection of my face and hair. Even to this day, I tend to stare at my image where I can. While I am still occupied with my looks, part of me pays heed to the changes that appear with time and age.

⚒

At the moment, multiple sclerosis has decided to destroy the function of my vocal cords. I struggle to produce any sound, and no one in my family wants to learn signing — even letters. Ergo, I am at a constant loss. I literally have to scream when I try to communicate.

When the caregiver came, and I was ready for the second part of my shower (soap, shampoo, final rinse), I told my brother (between gasps and sighs) to tell my caregiver not to dry my hair when the shower was over.

At this point, my brother sort of smirked in a ridiculing way. History: Multiple sclerosis (MS) had taken away the fine motions of my hands; this was coupled with an intention tremor. As a result, I was unable to brush or

3

comb my hair. This was disheartening to me and challenged my confidence in my own presentation to the world.

As a result, I quickly mastered the "art" of simultaneously drying and combing shorter hair with my towel. This, my friends, became the highlight of my shower. I would go through an entire shower to "fix" my hair. (And feel clean).

For my brother, who was aloof from my daily struggles and victories, my request was rather dumb; he made it clear with his sarcastic smile. The caregiver, too, smiled, but there was no meaning behind that smile.

The moment passed, and life moved forward. The day was young, and many more *such* things would appear.

In life, often, the smaller things help build ourselves, our confidence. These smaller things happen to be unique to us — maybe not the entire human race. However, people tend not to understand individual traits. More often than not, misunderstanding and judgment is hidden under the cloak of a smile.

Life continues — *even with the bittersweet pain of the smile.*

2.
DROOL

At the end of 2001, I decided to leave my initial college program to focus on my recent diagnosis of multiple sclerosis. Being 21, innocent, and a bit stupid, I had resolved to be the first person in the world to find a cure for the disorder in China, where not even a word of the language was familiar. Stupid.

At some point in my random life in China, I had worked illegally enough to earn sufficient money to organize an expense-paid trip to Hong Kong. It had become an interest simply because I was feeling confident and adventurous. The rich, modern, tropical paradise was certainly very attractive to my young mind.

Long story shortened for the purpose of this chapter, I came across a Chinese medical program, and realized that my search was utterly useless. The China trip didn't amount to anything but money spent and some unnecessary exotic experiences. If I didn't have multiple sclerosis, I might have enjoyed them more.

It is this experience that captures the essence of this chapter. Here goes:

Perhaps around 2006, I decided to live life. At the time, Hong Kong was life, and life was calling me.

Yet, as excited as I was, I decided to keep a friend with me for safety reasons. In an unknown environment, I would say, it is just wiser to have and maintain a reliable support system. Here, one can miss the trustworthy companionship of a family member. Of my choices was an idiot by the name of Stupid Quack. (Most certainly, this is not his name, but I do not find great gain in defaming individuals.)

Stupid Quack (SQ, I will call him) was, and likely still is, the human embodiment of utter nuisance. Against my sound tendencies, I chose him to be *that* support system, because he was readily available. I think, my only complaint about the entire trip was *that I took him — even if it was selfish.*

Initially, there was a 28-hour train ride from the city of Suzhou in the Western Province of Jíangsu to Guangzhou in the Southern

Province of Guangdong. (I hope I said them right.) In this train ride, SQ and I solidified a *pointless and meaningless* relationship.

Unlike American society, a plethora of cultures seem to support male intimate activities. Indian society is one such example; this is not meant to promote homosexuality, but certain actions may mimic suggestive behaviors. I am aware of this, and used to it.

In the long ride to South China, the scenery was either boring or industrial. There were few things that grabbed our attention. In this light, we inevitably fell asleep on the metallic bench assigned to us.

While I sat upright with my head bent down, SQ decided to lie down with his head on my lap turned toward my crotch. Moving away was futile, because he moved his head back even less comfortably. Furthermore, I was quite sleepy, and I didn't want to ruin my slumber.

At approximately eight in the morning, the train took a quick halt, maybe an hour prior to entering Guangzhou. People were beginning to stand up to check their overhead compartments. I had nothing to check; I had brought with me my handheld video camera — I hung it on my neck.

I stood up to stretch, and SQ moved with a rather loud moan. I looked down at him in ridicule.

And then.

And then—

Along with a slightly corpulent Southern Chinese woman, I noticed I was covered with saliva exactly where SQ had laid his head. I felt wet and very dirty. SQ had, apparently, managed to drool on me as he slept.

She kept staring at my crotch and him, simultaneously. A big smile on her face made the entire experience extremely frustrating and embarrassing. SQ, slightly awake, was somewhat amused. I began to wonder whether the situations I would face on this trip may all be of this, um, nature.

3.
COW EGGS

Another time in China, prior to my Hong Kong trip, I had *a rather pointless* experience — memorable, but pointless.

To learn colloquial Chinese (Mandarin), I took the help of a local Chinese teacher and her good friend. The two of them were happy, I think, to be associated with an international student. They were helpful in a plethora of ways — knowing where things are and how to find them.

The food was different, and utensils were not natural to my American upbringing. The culture was much more structured than Chinese culture in America, but this was not unexpected. Overall, (surprise) China was not America.

I adapted easily to Chinese society; after all, I had no intention of challenging it. Their ways were very respectful. Almost every ride in public transportation, children or young adults, yielded their seats to senior citizens — without being asked to do so. I was inspired to do it, and when I gave my seat away to an elderly man, he was a bit surprised (perhaps, because I was a foreigner (*waiguoren*)). I felt that I had done something good.

Chinese society offered me many simple ways of learning how to be a better person. This is something American society does not have, blatantly. I sort of miss that.

On the flip side, there were fewer positive things about day-to-day life. I was never able to find public toilets. The dirty, paid bathrooms did not carry toilet paper. Bathing wasn't too common, and there always was a bit of a stench.

⚔ ⚔

In this, my teacher and her friend took me to an open cafeteria, where I could enjoy some local dishes. They were happy to bring me here. However, I was sure to tell them that I am vegetarian *by religion*; I noticed that, while the general population does not have much importance dedicated to organized religions, they do respect people's religious beliefs.

There were few times that I felt confident in the country — the people were very friendly, but they *still* were never mine. No matter how comfortable I made myself, I *never* became Chinese. I was always a foreigner to them, *and to myself.* —

The cooks brought out, what they considered, a delicacy — what *they* considered. On a large tray, there were two large eggs. The eggs were white with large brown-and-yellow spots all over them. Maybe, there were green lines throughout the shell. Verdict: *that* had absolutely no right to enter my mouth.

Quick lesson in Chinese:

Chi pronounced like chi in chicken, is the Chinese root for chicken. Chi+rou (pronounced: row) is chicken [meat].

I would say (in Mandarin) that I don't eat "rou" because I am a vegetarian.

In Mandarin, chi+dan (dan pronounced like *than*) refers to the eggs that come from chicken.

Now, let's take this a step further.

"Niu" (pronounced like knee-oh) means cow. Ergo, niu-rou means cow meat or beef.

⇥ ⇤

When I looked at the eggs, I almost choked. (I don't usually like eggs or their taste.) The cafeteria ladies were proud of what they had prepared, *al contraire.* I was somewhat in an awkward situation.

I couldn't hold back. I finally had to speak up about the weird egg meal.

"Zhi shi shenme?" I asked. (*What is this?*) "Niu-dan," I concluded. (*Cow egg.*) I touched one, as if it were something alien. *To me, it was.*

Don't get me wrong; I know there is no such thing as a cow egg. However, if there was...

My teacher and her friend laughed at my comment and regarded it as something humorous with a little touch of sarcasm. This was not so much the case for the cafeteria workers. Upon receiving the returned eggs, they harbored smiles laced with disappointment. My teacher suggested that we leave the establishment, and eat elsewhere.

4.
STROKE

L et me tell you about my mom. She was mine, and maybe she was attached with other family.

In her life, she suffered three strokes. Each one of them was devastating; her recovery was tedious, and medical professionals wrongfully guaranteed that she would not be able to talk or walk. My brother and I, I guess, extracted a seemingly full recovery out of her each time.

Her maiden family was rather inactive in her recovery. I don't know how their supportive gestures would have expedited or significantly changed the outcome of her situation.

During her third stroke, she was taken to the hospital by my father. I was home from school, and I went with Dad. When we reached the hospital, she was very frightened of the uncertainty that awaited her in the immediate future. Before being sedated by members of the emergency medical staff, she began to wail out of utter agony and fear.

I could do nothing but cry like a helpless child — so this is what I did. I saw her tears as my own, and I felt the fear — not mother-for-son, but the other way around. For the moment, I *so* wanted to be the comfort she needed.

I lost track of passing minutes and hours, and my uncle, her brother, *finally* showed. I was genuinely not pleased with his late arrival. He came with an intention to take over the entire situation.

Upon his arrival, the doctor (in charge) came to speak with us. He wanted to know about my mom's background and medications. Living at home, I was aware of this, prepared to provide this information.

Before I could say anything, my uncle *tried to portray himself as an expert* on the matter. Understanding that it was his sister, I sort of "stepped back" to let him speak. However, I did not understand *how* he could possibly speak so confidently on *things that he had never seen.*

Most Asian cultures tend to take *respect* to another level. Sometimes, *we* tend to overlook actions or activities with unnecessary respect given to trivial factors like age or arbitrary status. Often, at this point, ego or lack of knowledge spearheads any proceeding activity. Unsurprisingly, this is a downfall of cultures that mimic the unnecessary rituals of cultures like the Indian culture.

⚒

In his description to the doctor, he mentioned my mother's previous strokes and her diabetes. Then, out of nowhere, he mentioned my mother's use of *water pills*. This would have been very helpful information *if she did indeed use them*.

A water pill, according to an uncomplicated Google search, is known as a diuretic. In simple words, it increases the output of urine. My mother never used a diuretic, and, in retrospect, I never witnessed the need for one.

My uncle was adamant that her use was, perhaps, significant. I could not interrupt him to make any case; his demeanor had convinced the medical professionals that I was of lesser importance.

I looked at her lying on the stretcher, and paused. At some point, my entire body was protected by the shield of her ailing body; it fought for me, sustained me through thick and thin — it loved me.

On May 1, 2021, she never woke up in the morning after a stroke that happened in her sleep. I could not smile when I looked at her. However, I wanted to leave her happily with a higher power.

5.
STROKE CONT'D.

I can't stop writing about my mother; remembering her, for me — I suppose — is not much different from a drug. Yet, her memories seldom produce fulfilling smiles. They're complicated, complicated beyond understanding.

We never really forget our loved ones; their memories are too real.

I wanted *to dwell in my mother's memories for some time. I don't know about everyone, but I like that I can miss people. I like that I once felt something for them, whoever they may have been. The memories may not result in fulfilling smiles, but some reactions to moments may lead to smirks.*

One can say that remembering a past individual and their presence in memories is sort of like *flirting with smiles*. It is never certain when laughter approaches a sea of tears. Smiles turn sour, and life's play becomes rather foul.

When I grew to the age where I learned what it meant to cherish my mother, life riddled her with a plethora of issues. I knew not how to solve any of them. My smile was burdened by the weight of the future.

Contemporaneous to her own medical issues were the unhelpful and, often, unnecessary gestures of her own family. While there was no bad faith, we were often left confounded by doubt or equivocal motives. At times, my mother found herself at odds with her own family — making smiling a bit difficult.

Yet, (sigh) this is a history best left to the pages of a pondersome saga.

6.
HUMAN

C ontrary to what my parents wanted, I formed an aversion instead of an affinity with the field of medicine in life.

Hours with medical professionals resulted in two things: a.) a hefty bill and b.) no viable solution for my troubles. Over time, my value for the increasingly non-functional system had diminished greatly.

Like a good child of Indian origin, the economic and professional aim of my parents was to establish a strong foothold for me in a relatively stable and economically prosperous medical field. Little did any of us know that multiple sclerosis would be life's restrictive challenge — that I would be a carrier of that medical field's defeat.

The result? I developed an interest in the *human* aspect of life. Where and when humans can be humans, I can love them. Inside the mess I call my body, I am but a structure of so many organs, ones that can not individually express the height of love.

I took an interest in *human* things, things that I could touch, sense, feel, and to which I could attach myself. I learned how to express my feelings in languages spoken by humans; I learned to gather thoughts in various settings; I learned to dream with children; l learned to laugh while shedding tears.

However, medical school remains aloof from me. I can't see what it does for me, except constantly remind me of issues that can't be resolved. I refuse to dream of worries and failure.

In China, I left a world of faults to open my horizons to a new realm. I marched around a random tree for over an hour telling my parents, in America, that I no longer was interested in pursuing the, for me, unproductive medical field. This, likely, was not what they wanted to hear, but I was an ocean away; I had time to gather and rebuild myself.

They were reluctantly supportive, but I highly doubt they were dawning a very happy smile.

Today, my multiple sclerosis is much worse than the time I was in China, and my postgraduate degree and experience have not resulted in gainful employment. I don't have the energy to wonder if things could have proceeded differently.

Yet, I *do* wonder if my mom's presence would have changed the bleakness of my presence.

7.
A RATHER PEACEFUL PRAYER

I figured, while writing about the range of smiles in my world, I should establish somewhat of a point of reference. In a world satiated with meanings and hidden meanings, it becomes very difficult to refer back to a comfortable and accepted foundation to which thoughts can securely or safely be anchored.

Some time ago, I was in a mood, I suppose, which resulted in a composition. I must have written it with an unplanned intention to add it to a book. It reappeared, randomly, as I had begun this book; after reading it repeatedly, I realized why it may be a good fit for this work.

A smile tends to be an outward expression of happiness — both momentary and long-term. Often, we welcome the gesture, and it symbolizes a stable and well-tolerated time in life. A true smile, I assert, is characterized by pure happiness — no strings attached.

This book, however, places its focus on corrupted smiles, dirtied by a plethora of strings — smiles that are ugly and complicated. It's not that they are unrecognized, but they are unnecessarily common, and burden life. Smiles that are "frowns in disguise," I call them.

I copied and pasted the following poem from my records. In a clean house, listening to light instrumental music, light a candle (and some incense, if you want), and *own* the following poem: (*Perhaps, it doesn't describe a sour smile.*)

⋖+⊢⊣+⋗

A Rather Peaceful Prayer

For the moments of darkness and the winter wind, I wish you a ray of the light of the summer sun.

By Kunal Vyas

The day awaits your conscious breath and the range of your patience. I wish you a long night's rest and the resilience to carry today's burdens.

Tears of joy are as powerful as tears of relief. I wish your tears of pain dry very quickly, so visions of joy are visible in a promising horizon.

I wish the food on your plate replenishes both your body and your mind. That what remains helps you feed the hunger and quench the thirst of a million others.

The day presents worry as it does excitement. I wish upon you the strength to endure both and realize that these things will come and go as the waves of the ocean very briefly visit the shore.

As the sun journeys toward the evening, houses tend to become homes. I hope your home awaits you, misses you, and gives you a comforting respite.

The earlier hours of your day inevitably create many a memory. I wish your memories weigh less than you, create no new walls in your home.

As the sun journeys beyond your sky, I wish lights fill your darkness, and warmth is a well-known comfort.

That your slumber is satisfying and the blanket of the night is a lullaby from a cherished childhood, I wish you so much.

Life remains beautiful; tender dreams help realities smile.

8.
AUNTS

My life's history simply cannot be told without allocating some moments to my aunts. Some, more than others, seemed "to carry the torch" in a race to *I don't know where*. However, we made it, *and I have something to tell somebody's children.*

When I consider the times I have spent with one of my favorite aunts, I realize and learn, introspectively, far more about myself than my moments with her have taught me. The freedom to explore one's own free spirit becomes infinitely more possible when judgment and restriction are not limited by embarrassment and shame.

My liking pulls me toward an environment of fun and growth. Sometimes, we find this outside the immediate family. My aunts were and are *far* enough from the boundaries of *strict* relationships.

Without mentioning too much, JV, I will call her, for me, *ruled* the streets of Ahmedabad, India. It's not her money that mattered, nor did the extent of her luxury — it was and, I suppose, still is, her "happy-go-lucky" nature that attracts me.

Another of my memorable aunts was my father's elder brother's wife. She was my mother's *jolliest* nemesis. Archita Kaki (*Kaki is the Gujarati term for a person's father's brother's wife*) harbored a very strong and, at times, belligerent personality. She seemed to be rather proud of being the older of the two daughters-in-law of my father's immediate family.

For some unknown reason, this gave her the right to quarrel with my mother regarding everything that bothered to exist under the sun. Conversely, my mother was no less of a "firecracker." It sometimes seemed to me that both of them were created to metaphorically battle one another.

Yet, they were lovable in their own ways. My aunt was utterly addicted to popcorn and imagined that she was a famous actress; every once in a while, you could see the passion when she was getting ready in front of a mirror. My mother was not so dreamy; however, she had her favorite actresses.

In her younger years, my aunt was very thin, and resembled a famous Indian actress by the name of Nanda. Her genetics added pounds to her as she got older. Both my mother and her passed due to some form of stroke or heart condition. Here is something to remember, though: one person's smile often equated to the other's frown. This was annoying, but maybe simultaneously funny — not for them, I'm sure.

I remember, when I was much younger, I was visiting India with my parents. There's about a ten-and-a-half-hour difference between America and there — them being ahead. Over there, in the heat of the summer afternoon, many people take a nap. (At 45° C, we had no air conditioning, only ceiling fans and open windows. I was five or six and utterly bored and hot.)

I couldn't fall asleep in the heat, and there was nothing to do. In my childhood mind, I decided that I should find a way to keep busy until the night. *The only way I could do this was to go to the zoo. Yes. Furthermore, my half-asleep kaki would necessarily take me.*

Upon trying to wake her multiple times from her afternoon laze, she continued to give me vague responses — this was not working for me. So, I told her that I would pour cold water on her head if she didn't wake up. In response, she mumbled something unintelligible.

Then, I proceeded to the fridge to retrieve a bottle of cold, *boiled* water; the fate of the middle-aged woman's head was set.

Result: the woman was a bit annoyed; *I had given her ample fore-warning.* I did end up going to the city's zoo. The rest of the day went as hoped, *and I knew how to do it again.*

⇥╂╀⇤

My previously mentioned aunts are (and were) from different sides of my family. The previous is my late mother's cousin, and the latter was her sister-in-law. One can guess the difference in relations. My relationship with both was fulfilling in unique ways.

While the previous made me smile in innocent ways, Archita Kaki was a little different. With her, I smiled, perhaps, at certain awkwardities. Among various elements of my family, she was the most volatile — maybe a little more than Mom.

9.
STUFF

The art behind smiling, I believe, requires no preparation. In fact, any smile *should* manifest as something natural and, perhaps, impulsive. In these circumstances, a smile is never coerced and does not require any form of planning.

A plethora of factors contribute to a natural smile: I have developed a list of things I find essential to the activity. This list definitely is not complete or exhaustive, but it is meant to make sense.

A.) Any individual is bound by the ease with which he or she is able to live life. To be able to smile with ease, there mustn't be barriers physically to the act. Here, I am not mentioning emotional or social factors that tend to hinder or prevent the ability to smile. Simply stated, there should be nothing physically limiting the action.

B.) At times, smiles are influenced by moral and social limitations. These situations include, but are not limited to, funerals or other overtly serious events, which place emotions in socially acceptable etiquettes. In certain situations, smiling is not supported or suggested, let alone encouraged.

C.) I put this here, because I thought I should have a "C."

So, what exactly is a *soured smile*? Let's consider this for a *hot* moment. The thing is, we all probably have experienced one, at some point.

Imagine: you have turned 20, and your father announces that birthdays will no longer be celebrated, because this is somewhat childish. He tells you that *you are older now and that you have grown past silly traditions.* In a way, he has complimented you, but also the smile is not really complete. *A little joy has been taken from the smile.* (This, my friend, is a soured smile. Perhaps, one may think of it as a *tax on the smile.*)

10.
DUPED

L et's go back to China for a moment. I learned so much about smiling over there. Smiles, I gather, are fleeting and can lose their purpose very easily.

Unlike the United States, the Chinese population does not boast of a prominent "middle class" but a notable division between economically rich and poor households. In this case, survival requires several diverse (*and sometimes shady*) methods.

I could say that *some of these people sell fleeting smiles.* It is when we look at *what we have really purchased, our money has officially been lost.*

I remember ample vendors, magicians, and roadside shops that extracted *yuans* (dollars) from unsuspecting people, especially foreigners — through crafty forms of trickery. I was duped so many times. It was disappointing, but eventually, their presence became normal for me.

In China, I was geographically closer to family located on the *other* side of the world. As such, my mom's cousin paid me a visit. He flew from Sydney to Shanghai, where I picked him up at the airport. Along with me, he also was visibly unimpressed with my living accommodations.

Unfortunately, neither he nor I could *change China.*

Since my mother was always fond of him and his family, I did what I could *to be like her.* I took my uncle to the market and bought (bargained for) a shirt for his son. (*I didn't know his son's size, nor had I ever met his son.*) Yet, it was something.

I took solace in the fact that he had heard me converse in a *somewhat* fluent Chinese. I know that he did not understand any of it, *but somehow,* the whole situation meant something important for me — *that I belonged to the world.*

In China, time had a habit of rapidly passing by. He, it seems, was only there for the duration of the "blink of an eye." In perhaps a week, he had to catch a return flight from Shanghai. It's like my vacation was over.

I figured that I would try to get one last thing for the Australian relatives before I bade him farewell. Being pressed for time, I started looking elsewhere for items to get as we were waiting. I could not find anything whatsoever.

Then, something caught his and my eyes, simultaneously. It was a man sitting on the sidewalk and playing with a toy that miraculously bounced back to him when he threw it in any direction. *It was a streetside vendor; I should have known.* I fell right into his trap.

When he threw the toy, a thin and almost invisible string pulled it back. However, the string was rather invisible, even at a small distance. For this reason, any spectator would initially be in awe. *I just happened to be that spectator.*

The seller explained the trick to me when I purchased the stupid thing. It was not expensive financially, but it cost me my integrity (in front of my uncle), I feel — resulting in, what I would like to call, a soured smile.

11.
PRICE

B eing a foreigner in my own world, I could not remember how to smile

I searched through dictionaries; I even flipped through encyclopedias for a while

There were, oh, so many things that extracted from me ample a frown

Without a smile, heavy are my feelings, and eventless remains my town

I think often about smiles and where they are

I can't find them near, I don't know if they're far

I worry so much about the bleakness of our world these days

Under the sun we live, but in darkness wander its rays

The brightness of smiles is too often hidden deep within puzzles or mazes

Lost in time, they disappear into several of the moon's darker phases

Sadness and happiness make their appearances at the roll of a dice

And smiles are expensive; I wonder — what, indeed, will be their price?

12.
TEACHER

T eaching and I always were "a thing." I just had a *knack* for the topic. I was never into showing the world that "my teaching prowess" was commendable. I didn't have too much support for my interest, since it wasn't *and isn't* something too financially stable in a fluctuating economy.

It frustrates me that one of the world's most educated and developed cultures places greater emphasis on financial gain and economic prosperity rather than focusing on intellectual development. Today, it appears that the Indian culture, my culture, is fading into historical glories.

At the end of my time in high school (2002), I took advantage of a course that gave me credit for developing my academic interests by shadowing a grade school teacher. Structured lessons in *Spelling* and *Arithmetic* took up several hours of the late afternoon. The third-grade classroom transported me to a time when *Algebra was yet to exist* for students.

My time in China, beginning some years later, was inundated with teaching opportunities. I was the teacher of different classes of young and older students. To some extent, they (and their parents) were happy to learn English from native English speakers. They thought that the education would advance their *caliber.*

I gained so much experience being at the front of various classrooms as a teacher or corporate trainer. It was so important that I dreamed that I would be one of those things in my future. In the weight of those thoughts, and worries of an uncertain future, I returned to the United States.

The freedom to choose a wondrous field of work in America is very difficult and a little disappointing. So many people struggle and even fail to present their very valuable talents and skills, because of rather expensive barriers and other pointless roadblocks. In different worlds: the best candidates for the job are often left behind for a *possibly richer one.*

Immediately upon return, I qualified for, and was hired as a substitute school counselor for a large Hispanic community and a records manager — all for a local school system. The job was a lead *out* of the work I had done in China, but I found myself communicating majorly in Spanish rather than Mandarin.

Teachers and parents would come to my room to admit their students to the school, or discuss various issues with children and performance. The caveat was that I was dealing *in a new language with problems that were very new to me.* To make it worse, I look Hispanic — so native speakers assume that I am well aware of their dialects.

I would wonder, every night, *how* I would *attack* the next day. Yet, I *looked* professional — I guess that was *preparation* for the battle.

One fine day, a young Cuban couple brought their daughter to me and told me (*from what I understood*) that she was having some problems with her classroom and classmates. Soon after, her teacher dawdled in. The parents did not understand English, and the teacher did not understand Spanish. Typical.

When the couple and teacher were seated comfortably, I thought I would open up our discussion or meeting with greeting the child. I put a clipboard with a blank white sheet of paper on my lap for taking notes. "Como te llamas?" I asked her name.

"Adel!" she screamed. Then, she grabbed my clipboard, tore out the white paper, and threw it behind her. The teacher did not show any surprise, and her parents seemed not to care. I didn't know *how* to smile; I missed China.

13.
MANIFEST

L ife is horrible when its most prominent adjective is "disabled" — or perhaps, it has to do with some form of destabilizing suffering. It's like: every natural smile *bothers* to exist with an expiration *period* — short or short*er*.

Things fall, primarily, into one of two categories. Are things in the current situation accessible, or are they stalwartly inaccessible?

To me, *stalwartly inaccessible* refers to those things that I can *not* figure out how to do, even working creatively with my medically-based restrictions.

My disability manifested toward the end of my college career. As I was almost ready to step into the professional world, *my leg broke*. Multiple sclerosis slowly took control of both my fine and gross motor motions. In life, I was satiated, in effect, with information that could not be used.

In this mess, relationships suffered and crumbled.

The comfort I felt around the extent of my own family and extended family gradually began to diminish. Perhaps, people who boasted of their *highly-educated background* were not equipped to deal with the troubles of an ailing family member. This structural dysfunction robbed me of one too many a smile. My eyes were more wet, and my moments of psychological respite had grown rather rare.

More than the physical symptoms of multiple sclerosis (MS), a person struggles to exist in a world *that he or she thought was very familiar*. Unfortunately, the realm itself becomes variably and *stalwartly* inaccessible, and a person is often left to struggle in a society of people who challenge the constant presence of a support system.

So, how do "soured smiles" manifest in this scenario?

As the author, I want to emphasize this part of the book. A person is prone to naturally smile for one of several distinct reasons:

1. Foremost, to outwardly express happiness.
2. Secondly, to outwardly express happiness at the cost of another's discomfort. ***

3. For formal purposes and social etiquette.***
4. To express friendly behavior and intentions.
5. Fifth, when goals or motives are accomplished.***

*** denotes where I believe that there is room for "soured smiles." What indeed is a *soured smile*? I figure that this would be a good time to explain the title of this book.

This book was my effort to touch the fleeting emotions that fill my day — those that add unnecessary burdens to my world. Soured smiles are ones that carry much more than simple happiness; like curdled milk, there's much more than meets the eye — it takes much more to carry and comprehend the complexities hidden behind the facades of those smiles.

Perhaps by understanding the presence and properties of *those* smiles, life would be simpler for everyone.

14.
COCOON

O ur world is composed mainly of our own stories and perspectives. For some individuals, the sun is *always* rising, and the grass is forever green. This is seldom the case for me; my world is not so easily positive.

I live in sort of a cocoon of soured smiles. Understanding my world, I can say, is like *fictionalizing non-fiction*. One can say that it is so much like imagining *impossibility* where *reality certainly exists — and then, efforting to overcome the created (and ridiculous) challenges of constructed difficulties.*

The resulting smiles reek of frustration and, perhaps, relief.

I find little time for being the superlatively positive person described at the beginning of this chapter, because I find minimal value attached to a non-productive realm. I mean: what *good* does it do me to traverse a land where the sun fails to leave? I mean, really. (I feel bad for chlorophyll.)

In that. I don't emerge from that cocoon as a butterfly, but as a moth. I find a light to, seemingly, endlessly pursue. Though, I *never* become one with that light — how frustrating?

⇒‡‡⇐

I conjecture that life is a journey from one smile to the next — from something more sour, maybe, to something a bit sweet. Life's situations necessarily and often leave us stranded amidst soured smiles and frowns; amidst these are genuine ones — to keep and collect.

We tend to focus *more heavily* on those things which prevent our *own* image of perfection. The more we do this, we accustom ourselves to *spilling sourness* on the ground upon which we walk. Our stories become unwanted, and our smiles become unsatisfying and even ugly.

The lemonade has too much lemon.

15.
SOURED

I thought I would dedicate an entire chapter to *Soured Smiles.* Soured smiles are, effectively, smiles that harbor the following traits:

1. Having a history/backstory
   There must be a strong reason to influence the outward presentation of a smile — even if it is slightly
2. Attached to an implicit emotion
3. Tied to something questionable
   Why and how can a smile be used to address a deeper, more complicated issue?
4. Bearing an inconspicuous disposition
   Perhaps, a bit secretive

⇥ ⇤

A soured smile, I assert, is just a *smile* with an adjective. Its plural form just happens to be the title of this book. Initially, I was going to place this section toward the beginning of the book, but I realized that it certainly helps when people are immersed into a world of *soured smiles* rather than eased in *step-by-step.*

When we smile, there's always *some* reason. That reason strongly determines the fate and, I guess, longevity of the smile. I often wonder: *do we actively effort to make the expression endure — when it is bound by definite time limits?*

In the case of a soured smile, the endurance or longevity is certainly affected by the emotional state that presides over it; this can be indefinite. A *soured smile* is also one that is easily remembered due to its infinite dimensions.

In continuation, the memory of the smile ties itself to prevalent environmental factors. In a way, soured smiles strongly rely on a persistent memory that affects the immediate and long-term environment. One can see it as a socially acceptable reaction to a rather complex and, perhaps, unfavorable scenario.

Soured, as an adjective, refers to a gradual degradation or dilapidation — leading to *denaturing* or *failure*. Naturally, smiles (purely) denote happiness, but *soured* smiles are a bit adulterated or corrupt. The presence of soured smiles is only something human; I am unaware if this occurs anywhere else in the animal kingdom.

16.
POST NOTE

Years ago, I had written a book titled "Failed Frowns." At the time, I had begun my writing career, and I was a bit unclear about the future — would I smile or frown more? (*Successful frowns* visit me much more often these days than genuine smiles.) Somehow, I had brought this book into my fate.

═+ +═

I wrote about both smiles and frowns, partially, to explore my *own* experience with both. Smiles appeared when I had the intention of writing exclusively on frowns, and vice versa. This was not a surprise to me, and it inevitably affected the direction my words took.

The fundamental feature of any smile is positivity — be it equivocal. The person harboring the smile is in full control of its *flavor*. The previous chapters provide a myriad of different examples of variously-motivated smiles. Yet, each, indeed, is a truthful form of a smile.

What I have realized, over so much time, is that the presence of smiles is, by nature, a deterrent to frowns. In some sense, you can say that many a smile can be related to *failed frowns*.

It's a bit funny to me, that this sounds like a "lead-in" to "Failed Frowns," which existed much prior to this work. I guess that frowns and smiles are related.

ABOUT "AN" AUTHOR

Who is Kunal M. Vyas? He is you and me. He is the prevalent thought of the passing moment; he's as much sadness and hurt as he exhibits felicity and bliss. He, you can say, is an eternal explorer of his self and a rather confounding world.

Between the years of 2007 and 2009, he completed undergraduate degrees in psychology and economics, of which *economics* was not expected. In 2011, a graduate degree from American University confirmed his interest in the field of International Development. In the end, these qualifications are nothing more than *haphazard* accomplishments.

Perhaps, all of these qualifications were necessary for some unknown purpose. Thus far, they resulted in the composition of this work. It is not certain, at this moment, whether more breaths will embellish a journey ending in another published piece.

On November 13, 1984, Kunal was born a Scorpio to Dr. Madhusudan Vyas and the late Mrs. Rekha Vyas. *Scorpio-hood* afforded him sharp physical features, wayward intelligence, and a passionate personality. Fate was jealous of him, and he suffered multiple sclerosis from around twenty-one years of age. Here, was the onset of a life far different from his plans.

Instead of saving a scary world, he was burdened with the task of saving himself — this journey, apparently, has persisted (and there is no end in sight.) He quickly got bored of multiple sclerosis and decided to pursue more interesting things. *Writing* continues to steal his mind's attention.

At 38 now, he lives to tell a tale, a worry, an annoyance, a regret; he likes to laugh endlessly at his own corny jokes. He enjoys the company of people from various backgrounds but likes to think (as a Scorpio) that they appreciate him *more.*

www.ingramcontent.com/pod-product-compliance
Lightning Source LLC
Chambersburg PA
CBHW032104020426
42335CB00011B/478